WHO EATS WHAT?
ARCTIC FOOD CHAINS

by Rebecca Pettiford

pogo

Ideas for Parents and Teachers

Pogo Books let children practice reading informational text while introducing them to nonfiction features such as headings, labels, sidebars, maps, and diagrams, as well as a table of contents, glossary, and index.

Carefully leveled text with a strong photo match offers early fluent readers the support they need to succeed.

Before Reading

- "Walk" through the book and point out the various nonfiction features. Ask the student what purpose each feature serves.
- Look at the glossary together. Read and discuss the words.

Read the Book

- Have the child read the book independently.
- Invite him or her to list questions that arise from reading.

After Reading

- Discuss the child's questions. Talk about how he or she might find answers to those questions.
- Prompt the child to think more. Ask: What other Arctic animals and plants do you know about? What food chains do you think they are a part of?

Pogo Books are published by Jump!
5357 Penn Avenue South
Minneapolis, MN 55419
www.jumplibrary.com

Library of Congress Cataloging-in-Publication Data

Pettiford, Rebecca, author.
  Arctic food chains: who eats what? / by Rebecca Pettiford.
    pages cm
  Audience: Ages 7-10.
  Includes index.
  ISBN 978-1-62031-300-8 (hardcover: alk. paper) –
  ISBN 978-1-62496-352-0 (ebook)
  1. Food chains (Ecology)–Arctic regions–Juvenile literature. 2. Ecology–Arctic regions–Juvenile literature. 3. Arctic regions–Juvenile literature. I. Title.
  QH84.1.P45 2016
  577.160911'3–dc23
                                        2015021757

Series Editor: Jenny Fretland VanVoorst
Series Designer: Anna Peterson
Photo Researcher: Michelle Sonnek

Photo Credits: Alamy, 10-11; Corbis, cover; Dreamstime, 18-19b, 23; Getty, 6-7, 15, 16-17; Nature Picture Library, 9, 12-13; Shutterstock, 3, 4, 5, 8, 18-19t; SuperStock, 1, 14; Thinkstock, 18-19tm, 18-19bm.

Printed in the United States of America at Corporate Graphics in North Mankato, Minnesota.

TABLE OF CONTENTS

CHAPTER 1

THE COLDEST PLACE ON EARTH

The Arctic **tundra** is the coldest **biome** on Earth. Winters are long and dark. The flat land is frozen.

Summers are short and cool.
The land gets soft and wet.
Strong, dry winds blow all year.

How do living things survive in the tundra? They **adapt**. Plants grow small and close together. This protects them from the cold wind. Animals grow thick fur to keep warm. Some animals leave in the winter. They go south. They return in summer when there is more food.

WHERE IS IT?

The Arctic tundra is in Alaska and northern parts of Canada, Europe, and Russia. It begins where the northern forests end.

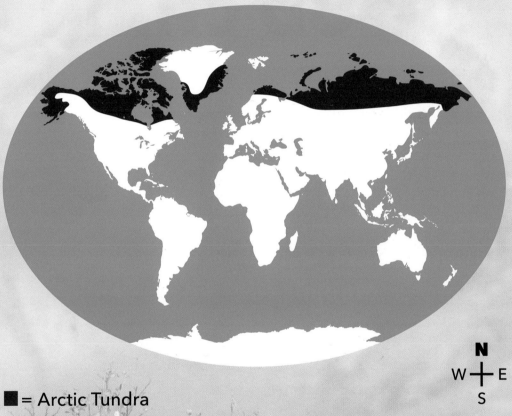

■ = Arctic Tundra

CHAPTER 2

THE ARCTIC FOOD CHAIN

Plants and animals need a lot of energy to survive in the Arctic. Where does this energy come from? Plants get it from the sun, soil, and water. Animals eat.

A **food chain** shows the order in which living things make and use energy. It starts with plants and ends with animals. Each living thing in the food chain is a link. Each link is food for the next animal in the chain.

lemming
(consumer)

plants
(producers)

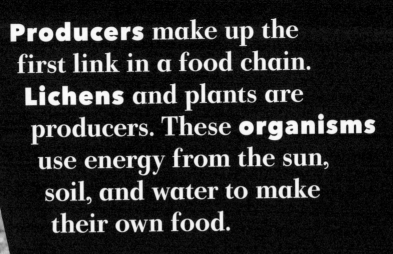

Producers make up the first link in a food chain. **Lichens** and plants are producers. These **organisms** use energy from the sun, soil, and water to make their own food.

Lemmings and musk oxen eat plants. They are **consumers**.

DID YOU KNOW?

Lichens are an interesting organism. They are part plant and part **fungus**. Lichens grow on rocks. They look like dry, flaky patches of paint.

Polar bears and owls are **predators**. They eat consumers. Larger predators will also eat smaller predators.

For example, polar bears primarily eat seals, another predator.

owl
(predator)

lemming
(consumer)

CHAPTER 3

FOOD CHAIN CLOSE-UPS

Let's look at a simple food chain. Plants grow on the tundra. An Arctic hare eats the plants for energy.

hare
(consumer)

lynx
(predator)

A fox eats the hare.
A lynx eats the fox.
In time, the lynx dies.
What happens next?

When animals die, **decomposers** such as **scavengers** and insects break down the bodies. The nutrients from the dead matter pass into the soil. This helps plants grow. So with the sun's energy, the chain begins again.

wolverine (decomposer)

One Arctic food chain might look something like this:

Producer:
Plants

Predator:
Lynx

Consumer:
Arctic Hare

Decomposer:
Insects

Let's take a look at another food chain.

1) Grass grows on the tundra.

2) A caribou eats the grass.

3) A wolf kills the caribou and eats most of its body.

4) Mice chew on the bones.

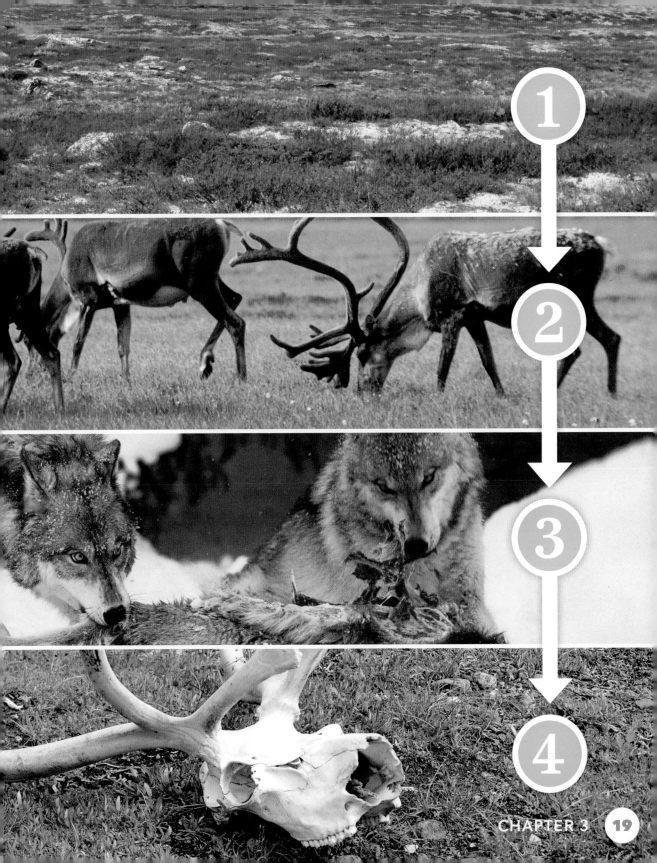

Animals and flies break down the caribou's body. It turns into nutrients. These will make the soil rich and help plants grow. The food chain continues!

DID YOU KNOW?

Global warming is changing Arctic food chains. New animals are moving in and competing with other animals for food.

ACTIVITIES & TOOLS

BUILD A FOOD WEB

In this book, you explored several Arctic food chains. Can you think of more? Get some paper and a pen. Start at the beginning by drawing a picture of a producer.

What comes next? Think about what might eat that producer. Draw a picture of that consumer, and use a line to connect it with its food. Add links to the food chain by adding predators and finally decomposers.

Now try changing one of the links by drawing a new plant or animal beside the original. Does the next link change? How about the link after that? Keep going, connecting the links with arrows.

Now you have made a food web. A food web shows the way a number of different food chains interact with one another.

GLOSSARY

adapt: Changing to better survive the conditions of a natural area.

biome: A large area on the earth defined by its weather, land, and the type of plants and animals that live there.

consumers: Animals that eat plants.

decomposers: Life forms that break down dead matter.

food chain: A way of ordering plants and animals in which each one uses or eats the one before it for energy.

fungus: A living thing, such as mold and mushrooms, that has no leaves, flowers, or roots and lives on plant or animal matter.

lemmings: Small, mouse-like animals that live in the tundra.

lichens: Simple life forms that grow on rocks.

organism: A living thing.

permafrost: The permanent frozen layer of soil beneath the ground's surface.

predators: Animals that hunt and eat other animals.

producers: Plants that make their own food from the sun, soil, and water.

scavengers: Animals that eat dead plants and animals.

tundra: The treeless land in the Arctic.

INDEX

TO LEARN MORE

Learning more is as easy as 1, 2, 3.

1) Go to www.factsurfer.com

2) Enter "arcticfoodchains" into the search box.

3) Click the "Surf" to see a list of websites.

With factsurfer, finding more information is just a click away.